ROAD TO GLORY

Percy Tau
ROAD TO GLORY

Jeremy Daniel

Jonathan Ball Publishers
Cape Town & Johannesburg

All rights reserved.
No part of this publication may be reproduced or transmitted, in any form or by any means, without prior permission from the publisher or copyright holder.

Text and illustrations © Jonathan Ball Publishers 2019
Published edition © Jonathan Ball Publishers 2019

Originally published in South Africa in 2019 by
JONATHAN BALL PUBLISHERS
A division of Media24 (Pty) Ltd
PO Box 33977
Jeppestown
2043

ISBN 978-1-86842-947-9
ebook 978-1-86842-948-6

Every effort has been made to trace the copyright holders and to obtain their permission for the use of copyright material. The publishers apologise for any errors or omissions and would be grateful to be notified of any corrections that should be incorporated in future editions of this book.

Twitter: www.twitter.com/JonathanBallPub
Facebook: www.facebook.com/JonathanBallPublishers
Blog: http://jonathanball.bookslive.co.za/

Edited by Liz Sparg
Proofread by Paul Wise
Cover by Johan Koortzen
Design, typesetting and illustrations by Johan Koortzen
Set in 13 on 18pt Bembo Std

Printed by **novus print**, a Novus Holdings company

Contents

CHAPTER 1	TROPHY TIME	1
CHAPTER 2	FAMILY LIFE	6
CHAPTER 3	SHOWING POTENTIAL	11
CHAPTER 4	IS THERE MORE TO LIFE?	19
CHAPTER 5	TRIALS	25
CHAPTER 6	MOVING TO PRETORIA	34
CHAPTER 7	BIG GAMES, BIG GOALS	40
CHAPTER 8	MEETING PITSO MOSIMANE	48
CHAPTER 9	PERCY TURNS PRO	54
CHAPTER 10	TRAVELLING WITH THE TEAM	61
CHAPTER 11	TURNING TWENTY-ONE	68
CHAPTER 12	SETBACKS	76
CHAPTER 13	A SEASON AT SPURS	82
CHAPTER 14	COMEBACK TIME	87
CHAPTER 15	BAFANA BAFANA COME CALLING	98
CHAPTER 16	THE GOALS START TO FLOW	103
CHAPTER 17	TRAGEDY STRIKES	107
CHAPTER 18	THE MIGHTY BARCELONA	111
CHAPTER 19	FOOTBALLER OF THE SEASON	117
CHAPTER 20	A NEW DAWN	123
CHAPTER 21	OVERSEAS	127

SOURCES	134
CLASSROOM ACTIVITIES	136
ORAL ACTIVITIES	136
WRITTEN ACTIVITIES	138
AUTHOR'S NOTE	140

CHAPTER 1

TROPHY TIME

Eight-year-old Percy stood on the halfway line of the brown, dusty soccer pitch and watched his team's defenders trying to stop the other team from scoring a goal. The setting sun was glowing so brightly behind them on the horizon that he could barely see what was happening.

A miskick from the other team's striker gave the ball back to his team and Percy quickly perked up. His teammates put together a few passes, then the centre-back rushed forward and booted the ball upfield. Percy watched the ball flying over his head and turned to chase it.

The ball seemed to hang in the air as Percy raced towards the goal next to a defender whose legs were twice the length of his. The goalkeeper was also running towards the ball. Percy realised there was only one way to win the ball and slip it past the goalkeeper. He would have to dive forwards into a sliding position.

The field was hard brown clay and full of stones that would scrape off the skin on the back of his thighs, and he knew it would be terribly painful. But it was the only way to score, so he threw himself along the ground, getting a toe to the ball, and watched it roll slowly towards the goals. He waited for the pain to hit him.

BBBBBRRRRR!

Percy's eyes shot open. He was flooded by a sense of relief as he reached for his cell phone and turned off the alarm. He was lying in his bed, 24 years old, and not in pain. He lay back in bed, breathing heavily, remembering the many times he had been covered in cuts, scrapes and bruises at the end of a match. But, thankfully, those days of playing on hard, stony pitches were over.

He turned and looked across the room at the shelf where the 2018 Premier Soccer League Footballer of the Season trophy stood next to two other trophies. The amazing events of

TROPHY TIME

the previous evening played again in his mind. Some of the biggest stars of South African sports and entertainment had been gathered together under the bright lights and TV cameras. It had been an occasion he would remember for the rest of his life.

Percy hadn't known what to expect when he got to the awards ceremony. He knew he had played well all season, but when people said he would win PSL Footballer of the Season he shook his head and laughed. He was just happy to be there.

So he was pleasantly surprised. Early in the evening, he had shared the Top Goalscorer of the Season award with Rodney Ramagalela of Polokwane City. Later, he was named the Player's Player of the Season. That award meant so much to Percy, because the players who had voted for him knew the game of soccer inside out and had first-hand experience of how he played it. Then, finally, he was named the PSL Footballer of the Season, an immense honour.

Three awards and nearly half a million rand in

prize money in one night! It was life changing. Only a few years ago, Percy had worried that his career was never going to take off, that he was an average player and would be easily forgotten.

Usually Percy was out of bed and ready for training at sunrise. But this morning, he lay thinking about what it had taken to get here – from childhood soccer games on the dusty, hard ground in Witbank, to Premier League games in the finest stadiums, and a glittering awards ceremony in a Johannesburg ballroom.

What a journey it had been! How had he become so lucky? And what was going to happen next?

Three awards and half a million rand in prize money in one night!

CHAPTER 2

FAMILY LIFE

Elizabeth Tau was sweating as she prepared a huge pot of *mieliepap* for the family. The sun beat down on the tin roof of her small, cluttered kitchen and it was unbearably hot. She thought that later she would go and stand outside, where the slight breeze might cool her down.

Elizabeth turned off the radio and listened to the distant sounds of her children playing soccer at the far end of the street, as she stirred the onion and tomato *smoor* that everyone loved. Out of the corner of her eye she spotted her youngest daughter sitting in the yard and playing with a handful of stones. Elizabeth tapped on the window until the girl looked up and saw her.

'Go and fetch your brothers!' she called. 'Tell them it's dinner time. The food will be cold if they don't hurry!'

FAMILY LIFE

The little girl raced off while Elizabeth sat down and served herself a small portion of *pap* and *smoor*. It was a bit too hot, but she managed to eat quickly. They were always short of plates and there was hardly ever enough food to go around, so she liked to eat a tiny helping before the children came in. Then she could tell the children that she had already had food and they wouldn't feel bad. Sometimes she had to go outside while they ate, so they didn't hear her tummy rumbling.

Elizabeth sighed and looked out of the window at the dusty mining town of Witbank, home to her and her eight children. Life was tough. Today, at least, they would be getting a bit of chicken with their *pap* and *smoor*.

But then her soccer-crazy sons burst through the front door, laughing and teasing each other, followed by their sisters. Elizabeth's spirits lifted. They were all precious to her; they were good children and she felt blessed to be surrounded by so much love. She got up and started serving.

'Mama, why didn't you have eleven children instead of eight?' Mogau asked.

'Ja, then we would have a full soccer team. Tau United!' Dumisani agreed.

'Nah man, never … Tshehla City.' Mogau shared his sister's married surname, 'Tshehla', because her ID book had been used instead of his mother's when he went to register with the Department of Home Affairs.

Everyone laughed as they took a plate of food and sat down to eat.

'We would be so much better than Witbank Spurs! They are bloody useless,' said Dumisani.

'Language, please!' said Elizabeth. 'We don't talk like that here!'

Everyone fell silent. Then Mogau spoke up.

'You are right, Mama, we don't speak like that,' he said. 'But I mean, have you seen our team this year?'

More silence as the children waited to see if their mother was angry or not. Elizabeth sighed heavily, pretended she was disappointed, took the broom and went to the door.

FAMILY LIFE

'I must agree. Losing to Amazulu last weekend? That was bloody useless,' she said as she went outside. The table erupted in laughter and agreement and the children turned back to their food.

For the boys in Percy's family soccer was their first love. They made sure that everyone was up to date on the latest goals, players and results.

As she swept the yard, Elizabeth worried that they were too soccer crazy. Maybe they were neglecting their schoolwork and other activities that would help them secure a better future. But she also knew that 'boys will be boys' and that it was a good thing they were involved in sports, not in other, far more dangerous activities. She was thankful that her sons were not like some of the neighbourhood boys. She hated it when boys she had known for years landed up in trouble or even in jail.

Inside the house, squeezed in between the people who loved him most in the whole world, seven-year-old Percy felt safe and secure. He smiled happily. He took a piece of chicken from his plate and wrapped it in a piece of old newspaper. He would give it to his mother, later.

Percy told himself that one day, he would make sure that when his family sat down at a table it would be covered with the finest food that money could buy.

CHAPTER 3

SHOWING POTENTIAL

It was a typical autumn evening and Percy and his brothers were playing in the street, running races, using stones to play marbles and chatting to their friends.

But it was a special day for Percy: 13 May 2002 was his eighth birthday. He knew that his mom couldn't afford to buy him a present. But Percy didn't mind. That was simply how things were, and it was no different for most of the people he knew.

His brothers had been doing him favours all day, making him tea, letting him choose the best seat on the bus, giving him some of their lunch. Percy was happy to be the centre of attention.

He saw his mother getting off the bus, home from work. She had a big plastic packet swinging from her right hand. Percy wondered what it was. As she walked slowly down the dirt road, the children rushed over to greet her and help her carry her things. They looked curiously at the bag.

'Don't touch. It's for Percy,' she said and lifted the bag up, out of reach.

Percy couldn't believe his luck. Something especially for him!

The whole family followed Elizabeth into the kitchen and waited impatiently as Percy took the bag and opened it carefully. When he saw what was inside, his jaw dropped, and he looked up at his mother in wonder. A brand-new soccer ball! He lifted it out of the bag, feeling the weight of it and ran his fingers along the seams. He had never seen anything more perfect.

Meanwhile, his brothers were going crazy with excitement. Lately, they had been playing with a useless, soft old plastic ball and had been getting so frustrated. They couldn't wait to play with the new ball.

After he had examined every centimetre of the ball, Percy handed it over to his brothers.

Percy examined every centimetre of the ball.

They grabbed it and raced into the street to give it a try. Percy stayed behind and gave his mom a huge hug.

'Thank you, Mama, for getting that for me. I love it.'

'You're welcome, son, I know how much you love soccer,' she replied. 'Now get out there and learn some skills. I want to see what you can do.'

Percy grinned. He didn't need another invitation to play. He sprinted outside, shouted to his brothers and immediately got into the middle of the action.

That new ball changed Percy's life. He had always loved soccer, like his brothers, but now that he had his own soccer ball, he thought of nothing else. He spent hours each day playing in a game or kicking the ball around outside the house and against the wall. Sometimes he even slept with it next to him.

Percy and his brothers attended the local primary school, Mmagobana Primary. Dumisani was five years older than Percy and already a star

SHOWING POTENTIAL

player. Mogau was two years older and he also played skilfully. Percy's teachers quickly spotted that he had talent and speed on the field and agreed he should play with the older children. The three boys dominated soccer at the school.

Every season, Mmagobana Primary played their rivals from the school up the road, Alex Mampane Primary. It was the most important match of the year. This year Percy was picked as centre-forward.

From the moment the big game started he gave all he had: he chased every ball and ran into spaces where the other players from his team could see him. He was fast, and the defenders on the other team found it tiring work to mark him.

Towards the end of the first half he was supporting a teammate in the centre circle, when suddenly he saw a gap behind the defence. He pointed towards the spot and the team captain slotted a perfect pass into the gap.

Percy sprinted to the ball, got it onto his left foot and made his way towards the penalty area.

He glanced up to see where the goals were. Suddenly the goalkeeper was right in front of him, with his arms out wide. Percy slammed into the goalkeeper, lost his balance and fell hard onto the ground.

WHEEEEP! The referee blew his whistle immediately and pointed at the penalty spot. The small crowd clapped and cheered. It took Percy a few moments to catch his breath, dust himself off and get back to his feet.

'Can you take it, Percy?' asked his captain. Percy nodded. He wanted this.

The goalkeeper was waiting on his line with his arms up, staring at him and trying to scare him. Percy stepped forward and placed the ball on the spot as the referee cleared the penalty area. Then he took a deep breath and decided where to shoot. The whistle sounded and he ran towards the ball, kicking it hard and low and to the left. He felt it was a certain goal. Then, to his amazement, the goalkeeper dived the right way, shooting out a hand and stopping the ball, which rolled towards the side of the posts. A hot

SHOWING POTENTIAL

wave of shame crawled up the back of Percy's neck. He couldn't believe that he had missed a penalty kick!

The crowd's cheers turned into gasps as Percy's brother Dumisani ran forwards and stopped the ball from going out, just in time. Dumisani turned to face the goals. Percy snapped into focus and faced the ball. His brother sent a beautiful cross over the defenders' heads, straight to Percy, who jumped up high, swung his left foot and volleyed the ball, mid-air, into the top corner of the net.

GOAL!

Everyone went crazy. Percy's teammates ran towards him with open arms and jumped on him.

'How was that, hey? How was that?' he shouted. 'Did you see?'

'That was way better than scoring a normal penalty, Percy! That was amazing!' said his brother Mogau, who ran over and high-fived him.

The Mmagobana team won the game 2–1,

thanks to Percy's amazing goal, and the triumphant team carried him off the pitch on their shoulders.

Later that night, as Percy lay quietly in bed, his brothers talked about what had happened, what they had done wrong and right and what they would do next time. Percy relived the match over and over in his imagination. He had never felt happier.

CHAPTER 4

IS THERE MORE TO LIFE?

During the 2006 season of the Premier Soccer League, when he was 12 years old, Percy became obsessed with Mamelodi Sundowns. They were the team to beat that season and every game they seemed to improve.

Besides being a well-balanced team of players, Mamelodi Sundowns had the amazing Godfrey Sapula playing in midfield and a young goalkeeper, Calvin Marlin, whose ability to keep the ball out of the net seemed almost magical. At the end of the season they were ten points ahead of their closest rivals and had qualified for the Confederation of African Football (CAF) Champions League.

On Saturday afternoons, Percy's family usually crowded around the old, battered TV set in their living room and watched the soccer games, shouting encouragement and instructions at the players on the screen, while cursing the poor quality of the picture. Friends from all over the neighbourhood joined them. Sometimes it felt like the whole of Witbank was crowded in their little house.

Elizabeth Tau cherished her weekends, when she was surrounded by family. But during the noisy games she often slipped away to her bedroom, where she folded and ironed clothes or took a well-deserved nap. She spent a lot of time thinking and worrying about her children and looking ahead to the future.

Elizabeth was concerned that the boys' obsession with soccer wasn't going to take them towards a good life. Few people become soccer professionals and she wanted them to find good jobs so that they wouldn't struggle to make ends meet. She knew how that felt and she wanted better lives for them.

Occasionally, Elizabeth would change the TV channel or radio station, hoping her boys would show some interest in a history or news programme. They would pay attention for a moment, but it wasn't long before they were energetically discussing topics like Ajax Cape Town's coach, Muhsin Ertuğral, or whether Orlando Pirates would ever regain their glory days.

'What else are you interested in, besides soccer?' she asked her boys at the dinner table one evening.

'We're interested in lots of things, Mama,' replied Percy.

'Then why I do I never hear anything but soccer, soccer, soccer?' she asked, which caused a burst of laughter.

'Should we rather talk about girls, Mama?' teased Mogau.

Elizabeth shook her head. 'I would rather hear about business or school – anything but soccer all day and night!'

'Soccer is an international language, Mama. Everyone loves it. That's why we're always talking about it.'

While all the boys in the family were keen

on soccer, Percy ate, slept and dreamed it. He was the biggest Sundowns fan of them all and dreamed about playing for them in a few years' time. It was Percy that Elizabeth worried about the most, and he knew it.

One day, Percy approached his mother while she was mending their clothes.

'You know, Mama, you mustn't worry about me. Professional soccer players get paid very well,' he said.

She nodded. 'They do, Percy. That's why every young boy wants to be one.'

Percy's expression was serious as he replied, 'I'm going to make enough money playing soccer to buy you a big, beautiful new house, where you can live in peace and quiet and where you won't have to work so hard.'

Elizabeth was touched by her sweet boy's concern. 'Thank you, my boy. I believe you. I know you're generous. But not everyone makes it.'

'I know not everyone makes it, Mama. But I am going to make it – to the top,' he replied.

IS THERE MORE TO LIFE?

If Elizabeth had looked up at that moment, she would have seen the determination in his eyes.

'That's what everybody thinks when they are your age, Percy. That's why you need a backup plan, just in case.'

'I'm going to play in the Premier Soccer League, Mama, trust me,' he said again, this time with more steel in his voice.

'Promise me one thing, Percy,' she said and looked him in the eye. 'Promise me that you will finish your schooling and get a matric. That's all I ask from all my children.'

In Percy's mind, he would already be a professional by the time he was 18 years old, flying all over South Africa and playing in front of big crowds. But he loved his mother and wanted to reassure her that he wasn't going to throw away his life. So he made a solemn promise that he would not drop out of school for the love of the game.

Did he mean it? He was determined to try and pass his matric, but he also thought that his mom would forgive him when he was earning big money in the PSL and she could stop worrying about him.

For the next few years, Percy worked as hard as he could, and he graduated into high school, ready for the next chapter of his life.

CHAPTER 5

TRIALS

Themba Mafu was worried. As the coach and manager of Witbank Spurs in 2009, he had a lot of decisions to make and questions to answer. He had to build up his squad of players for the upcoming season, he had to make sure that the fans kept coming through the gates to support the team, and he needed to do everything he could to get his team promoted to the Premier League. That's where the real money was.

Witbank Spurs had had an average season that year, ending twelfth in the Mvela Golden League. Mafu believed they could do better than that next season, but he had been forced to sell a couple of key players, to carry on paying staff salaries.

What he needed was to find a fresh, young player. Someone who would become capable of changing a game in an instant. He knew how much talent there was in the towns and villages of Limpopo. He saw it all the time when he attended games, visited schools or watched children playing on the sides of the highways as he drove past.

Mafu decided that he would hold open trials at the beginning of the season for anyone to come and show Witbank Spurs what they had to offer the team. Many young players dreamed of an opportunity like this to start their professional careers, but only a few ever made it. Still, they kept coming back for trials, and Mafu often encouraged the regulars, giving them tips and advice and telling them to keep on playing.

Of course, many players would never make it to the level that was needed to succeed in professional sport. Separating the good players from the great was the job of an experienced talent scout like Mafu. He knew exactly what he was looking for.

On the day of the trials, Mafu and his staff were down on the field by 8 a.m., setting up the

TRIALS

different training and fitness areas and a small five-a-side field for the players to use. When it was all ready, he took a deep breath and looked up at the clouds, hoping that it wouldn't rain and that today he would discover a legend.

On the other side of town, 15-year-old Percy and his older brothers, Dumisani and Mogau, had decided they were ready to show their skills to Witbank Spurs. The brothers woke up early, had a big breakfast of cooked oats, packed their boots and set off for the stadium.

'Ugh ... I shouldn't have eaten so much,' said Mogau on the way to the taxi rank. 'I feel sick.'

'Me too,' said Percy.

'It's good you ate so much. We don't have any food with us, so remember this full feeling when you are starving, later,' said Dumisani. 'It's going to be a long day.'

When the boys reached the field, they were pleased to see that only about twenty other players were trying out. They had played against most of them often over the years, and they knew what to expect.

'Jabu is here, Percy. You know how hard he comes at you, so be careful,' said Mogau. 'You can't afford to get injured at trials.'

'It's cool. I know how to handle him,' said Percy as he laced up his boots.

Percy was only 15 years old, a lot younger and smaller than most of the other boys who were there to try out. But he was used to that. He had always played against bigger, stronger players.

'Who's that?' asked Percy, looking at a man on the sidelines, as he jogged onto the field and started warming up.

'That's Themba Mafu. He's the man you have to impress if you want to have a future at Spurs,' replied Dumisani, and they jogged over to the other players.

'Your basic fitness is key to your success, gentlemen,' shouted Coach Mafu as they ran. 'No matter how good your ball skills are, if you're exhausted by the second half of the match, you're of no use to Witbank Spurs. Fitness comes first. Let's see what you've got to show.'

TRIALS

The trials started off with a few laps of the stadium, then some warm-ups and sprints to the halfway line and back. By the end of the fitness sessions, the players were exhausted.

After a short rest, they did some dribbling and tackling exercises, collecting the ball from the halfway line, doing a one-two pass with a teammate, getting to the edge of the penalty area and then shooting. Dumisani excelled when it was his turn, hitting a shot high into the top left corner of the net.

'That's what I'm talking about!' the coach shouted, and everyone clapped.

'Come on, Percy, you can do it too,' Dumisani said as he ran back to where Percy was waiting for his turn.

When he made it to the front of the line, Percy collected the ball neatly and sped through the obstacles quickly, but his shot was not on target and it flew high over the crossbar. Disappointed, he glanced over and saw that the Spurs manager was writing something down on his notepad.

The morning session ended off with a game

of five-a-side. Percy found himself in good positions a few times and was able to show his goalscoring instincts.

At the lunch break, Coach Mafu pulled Percy aside.

'How old are you, son?' he asked.

'Fifteen, sir.'

'Not bad. Not bad at all. Where do you play?'

'Mostly at school. And at home. With my brothers.'

'I like how you see the game. The way you're always watching the action. I'm going to be keeping my eye on you to see how you get on over the years.'

Percy walked off with a glow in his heart. He had been noticed, and someone who knew a lot about soccer had told him he was good. He knew he was too young right now to be considered for the Spurs team, but that was okay. He had done what he had set out to do.

Later that afternoon, they played 45 minutes on a full field, and Percy had a real chance to stretch his legs and show off his speed on the

TRIALS

ball. He wanted to prove that he could be a team player, so he dropped back into defence and made some good, long passes across the field, and tried to be unselfish in front of the goal.

Towards the end of the game, Percy watched as Dumisani scored an impressive goal down at the other end of the field. His brother was obviously one of the best players there, so it was no surprise to anyone when Coach Mafu pulled Dumi aside at the end of the day and spoke to him about joining the club.

The boys were so full of excited chatter that they barely noticed the long walk home. Mogau and Dumisani were both older and stronger than Percy and it had showed. Percy knew that being picked for a team like Witbank Spurs was unrealistic at this stage in his life. But he fantasised about when such a day would come.

This was a wonderful time in South African soccer. South Africa hosted the 2010 FIFA World Cup, which was a massive success. Suddenly everyone was interested in soccer.

ROAD TO GLORY

Disappointingly, South Africa didn't qualify for the knockout stages, but Bafana Bafana played well enough to show the world that the country had talent in abundance. Months after the World Cup was over, Percy and his brothers relived the great moments.

Then in early 2011, something exciting happened, which changed the course of Percy's life.

One afternoon, Percy spotted a nice new car cruising past. He watched it slow down and reverse towards the house. Percy was suspicious, so he called his brothers and the three of them stood guard at the front gate. A man in an expensive tracksuit got out of the car.

'Which one of you is Percy?' he asked.

'Who wants to know?' asked Mogau, rather rudely.

The man introduced himself as Mr Vilakazi, a talent scout for Mamelodi Sundowns. The boys tried to hide their surprise and politely invited him into the house. Their mother put the kettle on for tea, and they all sat down.

TRIALS

'So, let me cut to the chase,' Mr Vilakazi said. 'We've been watching Percy play, and …'

'You have?' interrupted Percy in disbelief.

'… and we think he has real promise.'

'You do?' Percy looked a little shocked.

'We do. We'd like to help you fulfil that potential by coming to train and live with us at the Sundowns Academy in Pretoria.'

The room was filled with a stunned silence.

'I'm not sure I understand,' said Percy's mom eventually.

'Your son has a future in the game, Mrs Tau. A bright future. We can help him get there.'

Percy felt as though he had been waiting his whole life to hear those words. It took all his self-control not stand up and scream for joy. At last, he was on his way.

CHAPTER 6

MOVING TO PRETORIA

In life, nothing seems to happen for months, and then it can all change in an instant.

After Mr Vilakazi's visit, Percy's life became a whirlwind of activity. Plans were hatched, bookings were made, money was borrowed for a new school uniform, boots and books. Finally, it was the big day, and he set off with his mother for the hour-long journey to Tshwane.

He was enrolled to attend Clapham High School, a Christian co-educational school in the suburb of Queenswood with a good academic and sporting reputation. All the teaching was going to be in English, so Percy practised hard to get his English up to scratch.

He was going to be doing a lot of travelling between the school and Chloorkop, where Mamelodi Sundowns had their offices and train-

MOVING TO PRETORIA

ing grounds, and his friends and family clubbed together to buy him an MP3 player, so he could listen to music. He was going to miss his friends in Witbank, but he felt ready for whatever was to come his way.

'Living the dream, Percy,' said Dumisani as he carried his brother's bags into the living room.

'Go get it, little brother,' said Mogau. 'You've earned it.'

'Thanks, guys, for all you have done for me,' Percy started, but before he could express how he felt, his brothers told him to get a move on or he would miss the taxi. They all knew that a victory for any one of them was a victory for the whole family. There was no jealousy and they all wanted the best for each other.

A couple of hours later, as the bus pulled into the Sundowns Academy, which was going to be his home for the next few years, he felt a flutter of excitement. It was really happening! A young player came forward to greet Percy as he collected his bags.

'Percy? I'm Keagan Dolly. Nice to meet you.

I'm your roommate and I'm here to show you around.'

They shook hands.

'How long have you been at the academy?' Percy asked.

'A couple of seasons. I was playing for Westbury Arsenal when the Sundowns crew scouted me.'

'That's a good team.'

'They are,' Keagan agreed, 'but this team is better. Wait and see.'

Keagan showed Percy the fields, the training facilities, the canteen where they would have their meals, and the room they would share, which was simple but comfortable.

'The room's a bit small, but you'll get used to it,' said Keagan.

'Are you kidding? I've got six brothers and sisters. There's more space here than I've ever had before.'

Keagan and Percy got on well right from the start, and their playing styles complemented each other, too. Percy soon realised that the standard of soccer he was used to wasn't good enough anymore. Young players like Keagan, Themba Zwane and Motjeka Madisha were already impressing the senior coaches. Percy wanted to be exactly like them.

Clapham High School was big and vibrant, and although Percy missed his old friends and teachers, he settled in quickly. The Sundowns Academy took up the biggest part of his life, but school was important, too, and all his coaches insisted that the players do well at school. Focusing on soccer didn't mean slacking off on everything else.

It took Percy a few weeks to adjust to life without his family. He had a lot of new responsibilities to work out on his own. He had to figure out how to do his own laundry, be responsible for his own homework and make sure that he was eating well.

Once he had settled in, Percy began to love the new routine. Late one night, when he and Keagan were chatting in their beds, he told his roommate about how, at home, there was never enough food to go around and his mother used to skip meals and hope no one noticed. Only now that he was away from home did Percy fully realise how tough things were for his mother, with many mouths to feed. He hoped that without him there would be a bit more food to go around.

On weekends, he took a taxi home and he and his brothers spent Saturday afternoons watching Champions League games or having braais with friends and neighbours. And on Sundays there was church with his mom.

In the last few months, Mogau had also signed a contract to play with Witbank Spurs, and Percy was thrilled for his brother. Spurs was an excellent team, and it was good to know that both Dumisani and Mogau were playing in big games, learning about being professional players, and making contacts in the football industry.

It was the beginning of the life that Percy had always wanted. Soccer was his focus. That was what he was there to do, and every day his belief in himself grew. He was building his skills and

MOVING TO PRETORIA

he knew it was just a matter of time before he would score goals against the best.

CHAPTER 7

BIG GAMES, BIG GOALS

For as long as he could remember, Percy had watched Ellis Park games broadcast on television. He had often fantasised about playing in the stadium that had so much history within its walls. Now, here he was, playing with Mamelodi Sundowns and standing in the Ellis Park tunnel.

Percy felt excited, but part of him also felt like an impostor. What was he, an ordinary kid from Witbank, doing in a place like this? But then his captain called the team onto the pitch, and he quickly snapped out of his thoughts and focused on the task of playing his best.

The Sundowns youth team was playing against the Wits University youth team in the warm-up game before the senior teams played. It was still a few hours before the main game would start, so there were only a couple of hundred fans in the stands, but Percy felt like he was playing in a World Cup final.

He had been at the Sundowns Academy for three months, working hard, learning the ropes, and he had progressed quickly. Now it was his chance to shine.

Wits University won the toss. They kicked off the game and it became clear right away that the Wits players knew what they were doing. They passed the ball around cleanly, they were patient in their build-up and they had skills galore.

In the early minutes of the game, the Sundowns players were guilty of standing back and ball-watching as their opponents put together a string of passes and fired shots at the goal. The Sundowns team felt overwhelmed, and Percy knew that if they carried on like this, it was only a matter of time before Wits would take the lead.

'These guys are serious, hey?' said Keagan, as Percy ran back to help defend against a corner.

'Serious as a heart attack,' replied Percy.

'We need to start playing or it's going to be a massacre.'

The Sundowns team were feeling unsure of themselves as Wits continued to control the game. Most of the time, Sundowns were stuck in their own half or chasing their opponents as they ran away with the ball.

The Wits centre-forward ran through a couple of Sundowns defenders, who offered weak tackles. Finally, the Wits player lost control of the ball and it bobbled to the Sundowns left-back, but his clearance was so weak that Wits won it back straight away.

'Come on guys, we're better than this!' shouted Keagan in frustration.

A few moments later, the Wits left-wing sprinted down the touchline, then crossed a perfect ball into the Sundowns box. The Sundowns keeper fumbled it and the Wits striker was waiting to pounce and stab the ball into the back of the net. A goal to Wits after only 12 minutes.

'Come on boys, let's get into the game,' shouted Themba as Sundowns restarted the game.

BIG GAMES, BIG GOALS

But it was no use. Wits kept flowing at them, over and over, running new angles every few minutes, sending long balls from the back, or expertly playing short passes as they worked the ball up the field. Sundowns were tiring fast and it wasn't long before the next Wits goal went in, and the next.

After 25 minutes of game time, the score was 3–0 to Wits. With over an hour still to play, it seemed it was going to end up looking like a cricket score.

Percy felt a rash of red heat creep up his neck. What was going on? They needed to get serious. He could see his coach fuming on the sidelines. The players were all too scared to go too close to him, in case he screamed at them.

Percy made up his mind to turn the situation around immediately. All his pre-game nerves and wonder at playing in Ellis Park had disappeared. It was just another soccer match on another pitch, and he refused to be humiliated.

A few minutes later, he picked up the ball on the halfway line, dodged a tackle and found himself with some space. His teammates were nowhere to be seen, so Percy took off at speed, running at the Wits defenders, who had been idle the whole game and weren't concentrating.

Percy feinted to the left, then shifted to the right and reached the edge of the penalty area. Out of the corner of his eye, he saw a teammate arriving, but he was in no mood to be generous. He was lined up perfectly with the goalpost and the ball was his. He swung his foot back and fired a shot straight into the bottom right corner of the net.

GOAL!

The small crowd cheered Percy's amazing display of skill, but for him this was only the beginning. He ran into the net behind the goalkeeper, picked up the ball and jogged back to the halfway line with it, impatient for the restart. They were still two goals down. What did they have to celebrate?

His moment of skill and brilliance energised the team. Suddenly they weren't intimidated by the opposition anymore and started winning balls.

He fired a shot straight into the bottom right corner of the net.

ROAD TO GLORY

Moments before half-time, Keagan gathered the ball and delivered a sweet pass right into Percy's pathway, and Percy slotted another goal past the keeper. This was more like it! Now it was 3–2 and Sundowns were back in the game.

The team jumped all over Percy as the whistle blew. Their coach's half-time talk was completely different to what it would have been twenty minutes earlier. Now they believed they could win it.

The second half of the match was an epic battle. Both sides were hungry for a victory. The small crowd had grown during the game and they were being treated to some excellent, open soccer. Lots of great tackles, some skilful saves from both goalkeepers and high-quality action.

Percy loved hearing the crowd roar as his team pressed forward. It gave him extra energy and determination.

With only ten minutes to go, Sundowns won a corner and lined up in the box. Themba flighted a perfect cross into the box and Keagan headed it towards the goalposts. The ball hit the posts, bounced back, and Percy stuck out a foot to guide it beyond the keeper. It was a messy goal, but all goals count. The teams were now level at 3–3.

Finally, the match ended in a draw and the tired boys walked slowly off the pitch. But Percy felt energised. He had scored a hat-trick, three goals in a single match, and he was over the moon. If he could do this, game after game, then the sky was the limit.

He hoped that his family had been watching the game. He also hoped that some influential soccer people had noticed what he was capable of.

Back in the changing room he could see that, after the game, everyone saw him in a new light. They liked the fact that they had a real striker on their team now. Percy knew that he wasn't 'just another wannabe' anymore.

CHAPTER 8

MEETING PITSO MOSIMANE

After the game at Ellis Park, word spread fast among the Sundowns fans, players and staff about the talented young striker Percy Tau. Members of the community started coming to watch the Sundowns Academy team play, share their knowledge and ideas, and encourage the young players.

Percy's favourite day of the month was when the youth team played against the senior squad. The last thing that anybody could afford was a serious injury during a practice match, so all the players were under strict instructions to take it easy and enjoy the game.

At the same time, the youngsters were always determined to prove that they could compete at the top level. Every young player on the field understood that if he proved he was the best, he

MEETING PITSO MOSIMANE

stood a far better chance of being chosen for the big matches. So, without fail, those games got very serious, very quickly.

A few weeks before he turned 17, Percy was playing against the senior squad when he spotted a familiar face standing on the touchline and watching the game. It was Pitso Mosimane, the new head coach of Bafana Bafana, South Africa's national soccer team.

Coach Mosimane had been appointed in August of 2010 after serving as deputy to Carlos Alberto Gomes Parreira, who coached Bafana Bafana during the World Cup. The South Africans had done well during those unforgettable weeks, and soccer was more popular than it had ever been in the country.

'Dude, that's Pitso Mosimane watching us,' said Percy, running over to Keagan.

'I know. But be cool. Don't freak out!'

That season, Sundowns also had a new coach, Antonio López Habas. Under Coach López, Sundowns had made their best-ever start to a PSL season and confidence was running high.

ROAD TO GLORY

The players were super fit, in good spirits and keen to impress the national leadership.

Percy realised that the new coach was visiting Mamelodi Sundowns to talk about some of the senior team players. But there was no reason that he wouldn't take notice of an up-and-coming younger star, too.

Percy had a good game that afternoon. He created opportunities for his teammates and showed off his pace with a few daring runs behind the backline that had the defence scrambling for cover.

But the game was dominated by the senior team's Katlego Mphela, who scored two impressive goals in the second half, one a diving header that flew into the roof of the net. Percy could see why he was the leading PSL scorer that season.

Seconds before the end of the game, Percy managed to scramble a goal across the line for his team, earning them some pride.

As the players were walking off, the assistant coach blew his whistle to get Percy's attention,

MEETING PITSO MOSIMANE

and called him over. Percy felt as though he was in a dream as he jogged over and smiled at Coach Mosimane.

'Nice to meet you, Percy,' the coach said, holding out his hand. 'You had a good game out there.'

Percy shook his hand. 'Th … Thank you,' he stuttered nervously.

'If you keep playing like that, Antonio is going to be forced to pick you for the first team,' Coach Mosimane said, looking at the Sundowns coach, who shrugged his shoulders and laughed. 'Then I'll get a real opportunity to see how you do at the top level.'

Percy didn't know what to say, so he waited while the coaches went back to discussing how some of the Bafana players were coping with injury. But Percy wanted Coach Mosimane to know how much he respected his coaching, so when he saw an opportunity he decided to speak.

'During the World Cup, I thought Bafana were really great against Uruguay. Your tactics were perfect; we just didn't have luck that day.'

Coach Mosimane nodded. 'I'm glad you understand that luck always plays a role on the day.'

'I do,' replied Percy. 'Some days we are the better team on the field, but we still lose.'

'That's football!' the coach said. 'I need to get going. Walk with me to the car. Goodbye gentlemen, thank you for having me.'

Percy was delighted to be able to walk with the national coach as the sun set over the training fields.

'Did you learn your soccer from your dad?' asked Coach Mosimane.

'No, sir. I didn't grow up with a father,' said Percy. 'I played with my brothers.'

'Ah, I see. I'm sorry to hear that.'

Percy felt he could trust the coach immediately. He told the coach about his family, where he had grown up, and what he hoped to achieve. He had the impression that the coach was trying to get a sense of who he was and how he would fit into the national team one day. He imagined

MEETING PITSO MOSIMANE

how exciting it would be if Coach Mosimane invited him to train with the national team. But when they reached the car, the coach just told Percy to keep his head down and work hard.

Percy knew that was the right advice, but it wasn't what he wanted to hear. He was ready to be a star! By the age of 17, the Brazilian superstar Pelé had already played in his first World Cup. That's the kind of thing Percy wanted to achieve.

CHAPTER 9

PERCY TURNS PRO

Percy's years at Clapham High were some of the happiest of his life. He found that a sense of routine made him feel settled. It was a huge improvement on his school back at home and he felt welcome here.

He worked as hard as he could academically, he performed well for the team, and he made some good friends whom he knew he could count on for the rest of his life.

There's nothing quite like the friends you make when you are a teenage boy, far from home. Percy and the other boys listened to music, gathered on the field to try out new dance moves, spoke about girls and felt as though they knew each other as well as they knew themselves.

Things were also going well for his soccer-crazy brothers. Dumisani's career had taken off. He was playing for Royal Eagles down in KwaZulu-Natal and he had made a big impact on that team. Mogau was a strong defender and had prospects with several clubs, so it looked like all three of them were on their way to fulfilling their ambitions. For one family, that was an incredible achievement.

One of the biggest nights of the year at Clapham High was the school dance. Everyone spoke about it for weeks beforehand, and Percy was as excited as the rest of his classmates. He'd asked a girl to go with him, planned a smooth-looking outfit and practised some dance moves with his friends.

'This is one night we're going to remember for the rest of our lives,' his friend Romeo assured him as they chatted at school a couple of days before the dance.

'Percy, phone call for you,' shouted someone, and he raced over to the phone booth that was against the wall by the tuckshop. Romeo watched as Percy tried to figure out who was on the phone. The call didn't last long, and Percy came back looking like he was in shock.

'What is it? Has something terrible happened?' Romeo asked his friend, worriedly.

No answer from Percy.

'Percy? Is everything OK?'

'I got picked for the PSL game on Saturday … against Orlando Pirates.' He couldn't speak properly but his friend knew exactly what he was saying. Romeo gave a big whoop, picked up Percy and spun him around. Everyone gathered to find out what was going on.

But no sooner had Percy begun to enjoy the moment than he realised that the game was going to take place the day after the school dance. Instantly, his world came crashing down. What was he going to do?

All his friends tried to convince him it would be fine. They told him he could party hard and then take a shower in the morning and be good to go, but Percy was sceptical. For as long as he could remember, he had wanted to be a professional soccer player. Now that the opportunity was right there in front of him, he had no intention of messing it up.

So, on the night of the dance, while all his friends were out on the town, Percy sat quietly in his room at the academy, polishing his boots and trying not to think about all the fun he was missing. He felt quite sorry for himself. But the following morning, on his way to the game on the team bus, he was pleased with his decision to skip the dance.

He had been chosen as a substitute in a game against the mighty Orlando Pirates at the Loftus Versfeld Stadium in Pretoria. A crowd of over 30 000 people would be watching two of the best teams in the country battle it out. It was vital that Percy be on top form.

Percy listened nervously to Coach López go over the tactics. He didn't want to make any mistakes, or draw too much attention to himself, so he kept quiet and hoped that he would get a chance to play.

Sundowns had a few good chances in the first half, but ultimately it was Khethokwakhe Masuku who opened the scoring for Pirates with a brilliant shot in the thirty-sixth minute of the game.

Sundowns fought back hard in the second half, but Pirates defended well, and they couldn't find a way through. Percy had nearly given up hope of playing, but in the eightieth minute he saw the coach stand up and look towards him.

'Percy, warm up!' he shouted. 'Let's see if you can find a way through this defence.'

Percy's legs were trembling a little as he whipped off his tracksuit and began warming up on the side of the field. He could hardly believe this was happening! Then the ball went out and the assistant coach signalled to the referee that they were making a change. He waited as the Mozambican striker Domingues jogged off the field.

'Get in there, Percy, don't be afraid, son, you've earned this moment,' said the assistant.

Percy barely nodded and ran onto the field. Even though there were only five minutes of the game left, it felt like an hour. Percy tried to settle in quickly and use his fresh legs to make an impact on the defence. But it was too little, too late, and the referee blew his whistle to signal the end of the match. A disappointing 1–0 defeat for Sundowns, but Percy wasn't too upset. It wasn't his fault and he had made it out onto the field to play in a first-class match.

On the team bus back to Chloorkop, Percy was glowing. As soon as he could, he found a quiet moment to call his mom.

'Hello, Mama? It's Percy.'

'Hi, Percy. Is everything OK?' she asked, concerned.

'Everything's fine, Mama. I just wanted to let you know that I played in a first-team game today. I made it, Mama. We made it!'

He waited for her to say something, but she was quiet. Then he heard a big sniff and realised that his mother was crying softly at the other end of the line. These were tears of joy, not sadness. He waited for her to regain her composure.

'Did you score?' she asked finally, and Percy grinned.

'I didn't, Mama, but just you wait. Any day

now I'm going to put my name in the record books.'

CHAPTER 10

TRAVELLING WITH THE TEAM

He didn't have long to wait. In March, Percy travelled to Durban with Mamelodi Sundowns for a match against Golden Arrows at the King Zwelithini Stadium. They were only one point above Arrows in the group, so it was an important game that would have some influence on the rest of the season. Once again, Percy started on the bench, and was forced to watch as his team went a goal down, then scored to end the first half of the game level with the opposition.

After the break, Sundowns turned on the magic and shot two goals, which took the score to 3–1.

Percy was hoping that he would get a bit of game time, and his hopes were met in the seventy-second minute when he was brought on to replace Lebohang Mokoena. He ran out onto the pitch and immediately got stuck into the game, working hard to break down the defence.

Seconds before the final whistle, Percy was standing on the edge of the penalty area when the ball deflected off a defender's legs and into his path. Percy was onto it in a flash and calmly slotted it into the goal, sending it millimetres beyond the fingers of the diving goalkeeper.

He was swarmed by his teammates as the final whistle blew. What a great feeling to have scored his first goal as part of the first team for the club that had done so much for him!

Playing for Sundowns was a huge honour and Percy loved it – not to mention the fact that he was getting to travel around the country at the same time. He had spent his life on the East Rand, and he was eager to see more of the world.

From Witbank and Pretoria to the Durban beachfront and Table Mountain in Cape Town – it was all brand new to Percy. He travelled in planes and luxury buses, stayed in hotels and ate different kinds of food – he loved it all.

He was swarmed by his teammates as the final whistle blew.

ROAD TO GLORY

For a young man who had grown up in a mining town, it felt very glamorous to be flying around the country on an aeroplane, staying in nice hotels, travelling by luxury bus and using world-class training facilities wherever they went. He tried to take it all in and be grateful.

However, he wasn't there as a tourist. The players moved between hotels, training grounds and stadiums. They had plenty of work to do, but Percy didn't mind. He soaked up all the experiences and felt that he was growing as a player and a person.

South African travel was one thing, but the excitement reached a new level when he was selected to join the team in a match against TP Mazembe from the Democratic Republic of Congo in a CAF Champions League game. The game was scheduled to take place in the city of Lubumbashi, a short distance over the border from Zambia. The second largest city in the DRC, with a population of about two million people, Lubumbashi felt both different and familiar to Percy.

TRAVELLING WITH THE TEAM

The Frédéric Kibassa Maliba Stadium was impressive, and TP Mazembe were known to be a very good team. Soccer is popular in the DRC and the stadium was full to bursting. Running out onto the pitch in the hot late afternoon, the Sundowns players were hit with a wall of singing, dancing and cheering fans.

Champions League football is in a different class from domestic football. Sundowns started off well but soon fell behind when the TP Mazembe strikers Rainford Kalaba and Mbwana Samatta showed how to score goals at this level.

TP Mazembe took the score to 3–0 in the second half, but Percy was able to make his mark towards the end of the game, which ended on 3–1.

'Well done, Percy,' said Coach Mosimane when Percy and his teammates walked off the field after the final whistle had blown.

'Thanks, Coach.' Percy was glad to hear the Sundowns coach's encouragement.

'It looks like late goals are your speciality. Last

five minutes, here comes Tau,' Coach Mosimane teased, and Percy laughed.

'But we need some goals up front, too. We don't want to be chasing the game for ninety minutes.'

'OK, no problem, I can do that,' said Percy.

He was disappointed that they had lost but thrilled to be part of the team. It was only going to get better from here, he thought, as the team boarded the plane back to Gauteng.

★★★

It had been a wonderful year for football, but Percy had different kinds of goals to achieve in 2014. Years ago, he had promised his mother that he would pass his matric, and in the final few months of this year, he put his head down and studied as hard as he could.

Playing professional soccer while he was at school meant that he had to make many sacrifices, and too often those were academic. But now Percy was taking some time off soccer to study. There were no more excuses. He forced himself to sit down and do the work and found that he quite enjoyed it.

When his friends teased him for working so hard, he told them he was doing it for his mother. But Percy realised that he also wanted to pass the exams for himself. He knew that a professional career in soccer cannot last forever. One bad injury and it can all be over.

So, he studied hard, wrote the exams and waited nervously along with the rest of his classmates for the results. When they were finally published in the newspaper in January 2015, he was overjoyed to see that he had a matric exemption.

Percy knew that his mother had dreamed about him getting a matric for a long, long time. And when it finally came true, she burst into tears of pride, joy and relief. Percy could see that he had finally convinced her that he would succeed, whatever might happen in his life.

CHAPTER 11

TURNING TWENTY-ONE

By 2015 Percy, Dumisane and Mogau were all professionals. They often travelled and hadn't seen each other for ages. But there was one date on the calendar that no one wanted to miss: Percy's twenty-first birthday.

You only turn 21 once in your life, and it should be memorable. Percy was throwing a party at home in Witbank, and everyone was invited. The extended family had been notified weeks in advance.

Percy drummed his hands on the table restlessly and did a little dance of excitement. He had just finished talking to his sister on the phone, and everything was planned for the big weekend. Percy had something special up his sleeve for the party.

On the Friday afternoon, Dumisani picked

him up in Johannesburg and they set off for Witbank. Dumisani had recently been transferred on a short-term loan from Witbank Spurs to Milano United, a club based in Cape Town. He had flown in from Cape Town that morning and hired a car for the trip home.

'Yho, this road brings back so many memories,' said Percy as they sped onto the highway.

'From your old life to your new life and back again, right?' asked Dumisani, and Percy nodded. 'It's the same for me,' Dumisani agreed.

'How's the new setup in Cape Town?' asked Percy.

'It's different. Lots to get used to, but I think it's going to be a great experience. What's happening at Sundowns? Why are you not getting game time?'

'Yho, bra D, you know how to injure a man, hey?' said Percy and his brother laughed.

But Percy knew Dumisani was right. He was spending more time sitting on the bench watching than playing, and it was driving him crazy. There were so many good players competing for positions and he was having a hard time securing a regular place.

Everyone was encouraging and told him not to worry about it, but Percy knew that he needed big game time more than anything else. His skills were getting rusty and his level of fitness was dropping.

'I've got to be patient,' he told Dumisani. 'Pay my dues.'

'Come on, man, don't be crazy. You're the best player in the team, in my opinion. They must let you play. Simple!' said Dumisani.

Percy appreciated the support. 'Thanks, although I think you may be biased. But let's not talk about work, let's talk about this weekend! Do you think Gloria is going to come?'

'For sure. And Zola and his crazy friends are also back in town. It's going to be awesome, trust me!'

For the rest of the drive home they chatted about the old days. Dumisani pulled the car onto the dirt sidewalk outside the house where they had grown up.

TURNING TWENTY-ONE

Elizabeth had been waiting expectantly all day and had cooked a big dinner. Things were a lot easier now that her children were grown up and earning their own money. After a long round of greetings with neighbours, the two boys sat quietly with their mother, eating and watching TV, and went to bed early.

The next morning people started arriving early. Aunts and uncles whom Percy hadn't seen for years showed up with so much stuff that for a second Percy thought they were planning to move in. His mother's friends, who had known him since he was a baby, arrived with baskets of food and began cooking. There was a spit braai that started early in the afternoon and Percy's friends from school and Witbank Spurs arrived with drinks and music in the mid-afternoon.

Soon the party was in full swing and it spilled out into the road. In this part of the world, where people often lived from meal to meal, word had gone around that there was a big party, and nobody wanted to feel left out.

Above all, they wanted to celebrate the

success of home-grown Witbank talent. To have a local boy play for the world-famous Mamelodi Sundowns was something worth celebrating, especially on the day he turned 21.

After everyone had finished dishing up and was getting ready to feast, Percy stood and went towards the microphone, tapping it to get his guests' attention.

'Hello everybody, please relax and listen for a second.'

Slowly, the guests settled down and turned to listen to Percy. A wave of shyness came over him. It was almost easier to play soccer in front of a crowd of thirty thousand than to stand up and speak in front of a hundred people.

'I want to thank all of you for coming and celebrating with me. I've known most of you my whole life and you've always been supportive, so thank you.'

The crowd cheered and raised their glasses in a toast.

'But of course, there's one person whom I need to thank more than anyone else … you all know who I mean: my mother, the one and only Elizabeth Tau.'

All eyes turned from Percy towards his mother, and she covered her face with her hands. She wasn't used to being the centre of attention.

'Mama, I know sometimes you were totally sick and tired of soccer, soccer, soccer, 24/7.'

She nodded, and everyone laughed.

'I know sometimes you prayed that I and my brothers would go out there and get real jobs.'

More cheers and laughs from the guests.

'But I want you to know that we made it. We all made it and we're all going to be OK. This is just the beginning for Elizabeth Tau's boys.' Percy reached into his pocket, pulling out an envelope. 'So today, as I become a man, I want to give back to you,' he continued. 'I went to the bank and opened an account for you. I put some money in there and every month I'm going to deposit some more from my salary, so you can buy whatever you want, whenever you need it.'

Percy's mom looked like she was about to cry. The crowd cheered as Percy went over to her and gave her a big hug. As he handed over the bank card his heart filled with pride.

'You didn't have to do that, Percy. It's too much,' his mom said.

'I didn't have to, but I wanted to, Mama. More than anything.'

They hugged again, and the crowd broke into song. Percy thanked everyone once again and went back to his table.

The guests danced and celebrated late into the night. It was an occasion to remember and Percy was so happy to be able to give back a little bit to his community.

The next day, his thoughts turned to his career and to how he was going to secure a regular starting position in the Sundowns line-up. He was ready to take his game to the next level.

As he handed over the bank card his heart filled with pride.

CHAPTER 12

SETBACKS

Percy woke up before sunrise and forced himself out of bed. It was cold in the small flat that he was renting in Pretoria. He dressed quickly, gulped a glass of milk and ran down the stairs to start his training run.

Outside, his breath rose in clouds in the icy air. He did some quick stretches and set off down the road. After a few hundred meters, with his muscles warming up, he began to feel human again and stopped thinking about going back to bed.

He ran through the quiet suburban streets, then past the taxi rank where commuters were already lining up for work, and down towards the city centre.

As he ran, Percy tried to clear his mind by focusing on his breath, but he felt troubled and

SETBACKS

he couldn't stop worrying. A year had passed since his twenty-first birthday, and things had not gone according to plan.

Although he was moving into the prime of his career with one of the best teams on the African continent, none of that mattered if he couldn't get game time. Something wasn't working, and he couldn't quite figure out why. He wasn't scoring goals or connecting with his teammates and he didn't feature in the coach's plans.

He was desperate to maintain his fitness, but he spent so much time sitting on the bench that it was getting harder to do. Sometimes he felt like giving up. Who was even paying attention to him? Did anyone notice that he was trying his hardest? It didn't feel like it. Percy's confidence was suffering badly.

That morning, he pushed his body hard, trying to force the negative thoughts from his mind. Coming into the home stretch, Percy broke into a sprint and ran until his lungs felt like they would burst. Then he collapsed onto the pavement outside his front gate, gasping for air.

Later that day, after squad practice at the training ground, Percy stood on the edge of the penalty area, lining up balls and shooting for the top right corner. He had set himself a challenge: he wasn't allowed to go home until he had hit the back of the net with five balls in a row.

His teammates packed up and left the field, but Percy carried on kicking balls until he felt that he could do it in his sleep. Finally, he got all five in a row and he raised his arms in victory, although no one was watching. Then his phone beeped in his bag. It was a message from Coach Mosimane, calling Percy into his office.

Percy had a bad feeling about this, but there was nothing he could do about it. He raced off to shower and made his way up to the office. The coach was talking on his phone, so Percy waited nervously in the hallway, then knocked and entered after he heard Coach Mosimane saying goodbye.

'Hi Percy, have a seat,' the coach greeted Percy pleasantly. 'How are things with you?'

Percy shrugged. 'Not too bad, Coach.

SETBACKS

Training was good today. I feel like I'm coming right again.'

'That's good. Really good.' The coach sighed heavily, and Percy felt a sinking feeling in the pit of his stomach. 'You haven't been performing at your peak this season, but I think you know that, right?'

Percy nodded. He didn't know what to say, and tension hung in the air.

Finally, Coach Mosimane broke the silence. 'Look, Percy, you know that I think you are a very good player. Ever since I saw you as a youngster at Spurs, I've been impressed. But … we need to be honest with each other. This season, something is off.'

Percy looked down at his feet and nodded again. Lying in bed at night, unable to sleep, he had worried that Sundowns were about to let him go. After all, he hadn't played a single first-team game all season. He thought he was ready for the bad news, but this was so much harder than he imagined.

'What I want for you is game time. That's

what you need. So, I've made a decision.'

Percy looked up, his heart in his mouth.

'You're going to go on loan to Witbank Spurs for the rest of the season and see if you can get out of this slump.'

'Witbank Spurs?' said Percy. 'But that's ... that's not even Premier League, that's First Division.'

'I know. But they know your game, they understand you and I think you'll be able to get back into form there.'

Percy was shocked. He hadn't seen that coming. It was a relief that he wasn't being transferred and that he was only going out on loan. But First Division soccer! That was going backwards in his career.

The rest of the meeting passed by in a blur; Percy hardly heard anything that Coach Mosimane was saying. All he kept thinking was that he had failed and that he was never going to make it as a professional player. He could barely stand the feeling.

When the meeting was finally over, Percy

SETBACKS

made his way back to his room. He didn't want to see or tell anyone. He just wanted the ground to swallow him up. He turned off his phone, locked his door and closed his eyes, falling into a deep, dreamless sleep.

The next morning, Percy packed up his stuff and told his teammates the news. They were surprised and sorry, but they encouraged him to work hard, telling him that he would be back in the team before he knew it.

To Percy the move felt like the end of all he had hoped for. How was he going to face his family and friends? They would look at him as a failure. He wished that he had been transferred to Cape Town or Pietermaritzburg or anywhere that wasn't his home town. But he simply had to get on the road back to Witbank and deal with whatever the future held for him.

CHAPTER 13

A SEASON AT SPURS

The Spurs coach, Themba Mafu, was waiting for Percy when he reported to the club the following Monday. He knew Percy was going to be disappointed. That was only natural. So his first job was to get his star player's spirits back up. He had to show Percy that this was just another part of the journey towards becoming a first-class footballer.

Mafu was the one who had first spotted Percy's talent all those years ago when Percy was a teenager. He had been watching the player's development carefully over the years and had come up with a two-part plan for the season.

One of the common criticisms of Percy was that he was 'lazy'. Mafu knew that wasn't the case. Percy had a real hunger for the game, but when he was not given the position of striker, he tended to drift around and wait, and that gave people the impression that he was not working hard enough.

So, the first thing that Mafu had decided was that Percy should switch out from playing on the wing into a more central striker's role. He needed to be more involved in the action and to be making more decisions in the centre of the field. Mafu had spoken to Rhulani Mokwena, a coach who had also worked with Percy in the Sundowns Under-19 team, and they had agreed that it was the right thing to do.

The second decision Mafu made was to get Percy a personal trainer; someone who would discover his strengths and weaknesses and get him into the best shape of his life.

Going back to where his career had started was difficult, but after a few weeks Percy began to adjust and focus on the positive aspects. He was going to be playing more than ever, and he could spend more time with his family, too.

But when he first saw his mother, he couldn't hide his shame.

'I'm sorry, Mama. I've let you down,' he said.

'What nonsense are you talking, boy? I've never been prouder of you.'

'How is that possible? I wasn't good enough for the PSL.'

'Don't say that, Percy. Don't even think that. This is temporary.'

'Is it, Mama? I don't know. Sometimes I think I must grow up and get a real job.'

'No, my boy, no. I used to think that but not any more,' she said.

'Really?' said Percy.

'Trust me on that,' his mother replied. 'I see so many people who are unhappy in their jobs, and then I look at the joy you and your brothers get from playing. It's a great thing.'

That was exactly what he needed to hear.

Out on the pitch, Percy began to get his groove back. He worked hard in his new central role, and he could feel his strength and stamina picking up. He also needed to become more of an all-round team player. It was something that the Sundowns coaching staff had asked him to concentrate on. So, he assisted his team and got involved in the game wherever he could.

After three months of intense work, Percy felt like a changed man. Running out onto the pitch at the Peter Mokaba Stadium in Polokwane one afternoon, Percy looked up into the stands and saw Walter Steenbok, a Sundowns coach who was there to watch him play. A few years ago, Percy would have tried to show some individual brilliance, but things had changed. Now he wanted to show that he was a team player.

It was an important game for Witbank Spurs if they were going to be promoted to the Premier League. Percy slotted into his new position, working the ball around the pitch, creating chances for the other players and finding space where he could. He charged back in defence when he had to and took his chances as striker when they came up.

Walking off the pitch at the end of the game, Percy glanced at the stands and saw Coach Steenbok giving him a thumbs up, which made him feel happy.

ROAD TO GLORY

Later that week, Walter Steenbok met with Pitso Mosimane. As a scout for Sundowns, he was expected to keep Mosimane informed about new talent and how players who were loosely connected to Sundowns were doing. He was able to tell the boss that Percy was now playing a different kind of soccer.

'He's moving easily, he looks great and his work rate is much higher than I can ever remember seeing, boss. It's like he's a new man.'

'That's wonderful news, Walter. Exactly what we wanted. Keep me posted on any developments,' said Mosimane.

The coach knew that there would be a role for Percy back in his team soon. He wasn't sure exactly when, but he was certain that Percy Tau would wear the Sundowns jersey with pride once again.

CHAPTER 14

COMEBACK TIME

It was 2016 and Mamelodi Sundowns were having an excellent year. They had dominated the PSL, ending the season 14 points above their nearest rivals, Bidvest Wits. They had won 22 games and lost only three out of the 30 games they played.

But Sundowns were also lucky. After being eliminated from the CAF Champions League, they were put back in when another team was suspended. Suddenly, they found themselves in the semi-finals, up against the Zambian club Zesco United.

When Percy had watched the earlier group stages of the Champions League games, he had found it hard to contain his different emotions. He was enormously proud of his team for doing so well. But he had also felt stabs of jealousy. He longed to be part of the team on their adventure.

A few days later, Percy was walking to catch the bus after a training session when a call came in from a Tshwane number.

'Hello?' he answered.

'Percy? It's Walter Steenbok here.'

'How are you, Coach?'

'Fine, fine … thank you. Listen I have good news for you. I've been monitoring your season and you've done very well.'

Percy stopped walking and leaned against a car. Was this the moment that he had been hoping for since that day in Coach Mosimane's office?

'We want you to come back into the squad. ASAP. There are some big games coming up and Coach Mosimane thinks you'll be a real asset to the team.'

'I …' Percy's voice trailed off. For once, he was speechless. He had to pinch himself to make sure he wasn't imagining the call. Eventually he managed to stammer out, 'Thanks Coach. I'll be there.'

'Great. I'll make the arrangements with Spurs. Just get back here fast.'

COMEBACK TIME

Percy wanted to jump for joy and scream at the top of his lungs. His patience was being rewarded. He had been willing to change and fix his game, and it was working. He immediately sent a message to his family to tell them the good news.

A couple of days later, Percy took a deep breath and walked into the changing room at Sundowns. He wanted to play it cool and act like it was no big deal, although his heart was racing. But, when the other players saw him come in, they started whooping and cheering as if he were a conquering hero.

'Percy! Long time, my man,' shouted Tiyani Mabunda from the back of the changing room.

'Too long!' shouted Khama Billiat, and Percy grinned from ear to ear.

His teammates at Spurs had earned his respect as hardworking and talented players, and he had been sad to say goodbye. But Sundowns was where he belonged, and he was determined not to let this second chance slip out of his grasp.

The semi-final matches of the CAF Champions League consisted of two games, home and away, and the first game would be played in Zambia. Percy was more nervous than he had been in a long while as he boarded the flight. The Zambians were a skilful, very physical team.

Sundowns had a few good chances to score in the first half of the game, but they were unable to convert them into goals. Then, early in the second half, Zambian striker Jackson Mwanza scored twice for Zesco in the space of two minutes. Coach Mosimane quickly made some on-field changes, bringing on Asavela Mbekile and Teko Modise.

A few minutes later, Percy found himself unmarked on the edge of the penalty area, and when the ball was played out towards him, he cut all the way down to the line and then tried to find a way in. Glancing up, he saw that the angle was tight but that he could squeeze in a shot on goal. He took the chance but mistimed his kick, and the ball went flying over the crossbar. The local fans who had travelled with Sundowns groaned and Percy felt angry with himself. He knew he could do better.

COMEBACK TIME

Moments later, Percy had another opportunity to go for goal, but his shot lacked any power and the goalkeeper easily collected the ball. To make matters worse, Percy realised that Khama Billiat had been unmarked, and in a much better position than him to shoot. Percy should have passed the ball to his teammate.

'Come on boys, we need that away goal!' shouted Coach Mosimane from the touchline, and Sundowns pressed forward again.

The clock was running down when Billiat finally managed to get the ball past the goalkeeper's outstretched arms and score. A loss by one goal to two to the Zambian team wasn't terrible. If they could win by two goals at home, then they would be on their way to the finals. It wasn't over yet.

One week later, Sundowns hosted Zesco at the Lucas Moripe Stadium in a must-win match. The stadium was packed, and tensions were high as the fans were expecting a two-goal win. Soon after the game kicked off, Sundowns took the lead when Keagan Dolly raced down the wing and sent in a beautiful cross. It was cleared by Zesco but fell into the path of Sundowns player Anthony Laffor, who beat two defenders, looked up and saw the goalkeeper was out of position, and struck a beautiful shot that kept rising all the way into the back of the net.

Only five minutes into the game, and the score was 1–0 to Sundowns. But one goal still wasn't enough.

Zesco came back strongly, but they were unable to break down Sundown's defence. Percy was playing well; he knew he just had to be patient to score. And then, finally, in the sixty-third minute, his opportunity came when the ball bobbed around in the penalty area and no one could clear it. Percy rose up high, headed the ball cleanly and saw it hit the back of the net.

GOAL!

The score was 2–0 to Sundowns. During the last 25 minutes of the game, the visitors attacked in wave after wave, but Sundowns held out until the final whistle.

COMEBACK TIME

They had made it! Sundowns were into the final game of the CAF Champions League against the world-famous Egyptian club Zamalek.

At the end of the game, Coach Mosimane ran towards Percy with wide-open arms, gathered him in a big hug and thanked him for scoring the winning goal. Percy's goal drought was over, and his confidence was back. He was looking forward to seeing what Sundowns could do in the finals against Zamalek, with its fearsome reputation.

As with the semi-finals, the finals also consisted of two games: one at home and one away. The first game was scheduled for 15 October at the Lucas Moripe Stadium. The coach decided that Sundowns would play with four defenders and one big centre-forward, Khama Billiat. That placed Percy in the centre, playing behind Billiat.

Finally, the big day dawned.

Zamalek were famous for their flair and attacking skills, but on that night they were no match for the mighty Sundowns. Anthony Laffor scored the first goal for Sundowns after half an hour, and ten minutes later Sundowns defender

ROAD TO GLORY

Tebogo Langerman added a second goal.

After the half-time break, Zamalek made a bad defensive error and scored an own goal. It was 3–0 to Sundowns in the 2016 CAF Champions League final home game! The crowd was going crazy. Zamalek brought on new attackers, but it was no good and the game ended with a Sundowns victory, three goals up.

Back in the changing room, there was a stunned silence. The team could hardly believe it. Although there was another game to play in Egypt, it seemed impossible to lose from a three-goal lead.

One week later, Percy made his first trip to the Egyptian capital, Cairo, with the team. It was a thrill to be in such an exciting city. Cairo was huge and sprawling, alive with energy, noise, people and traffic. For a moment, he forgot all about football.

The excitement grew more intense and it was hard not to feel overwhelmed when the team reached the Cairo International Stadium for the game. The Zamalek fans were determined to show their loyalty to their team. The huge stands were teeming with people, and noisy, smoky fireworks added to the chaotic scene.

Coach Mosimane gathered his players in the changing room and tried to keep them calm. 'Just another game, boys. No different from any other you've played,' he said. 'Don't be intimidated by the crowds and the noise. Let's stick to the plan and play the kind of game we know we can play. I'm already proud of you guys. Now let's do this for the nation.'

The sound as the teams walked out of the tunnel was deafening. To beat Mamelodi Sundowns, Zamalek would have to get four goals, and they knew they had to score early. They turned on the pressure and Percy dropped back to defend alongside his teammates. He felt glad that he had learned so much about defence at Spurs. Sundowns pushed back attack after attack, and by the end of the first half the exhausted teams were still level at 0–0.

Sundowns were determined to hold on for another 45 minutes in the second half. Then

Zamalek finally scored their first goal in the sixty-fourth minute. The crowd went crazy as they screamed for their team to score again.

But for Zamalek it was too little, too late. Sundowns held out until the end, winning the 2016 CAF Champions League with an aggregate score of 3–1. They had done it! Sundowns were the first South African team to be crowned champions of Africa.

Coach Mosimane rushed onto the field and started hugging the players and lifting them up into the air.

'We did it, Percy! We did it!' he shouted, and Percy grinned from ear to ear.

'Thanks for bringing me back, Coach. It means the world to me.'

'You did the work, Percy. You deserve to be here,' said his coach.

Those words were music to Percy's ears. He could hardly believe that a few short months before he had felt defeated. Now here he was, on top of the world.

'We did it, Percy! We did it!' Coach Mosimane shouted.

CHAPTER 15

BAFANA BAFANA COME CALLING

Percy's excellent form was rewarded in March of 2017, when he got called up to join the national squad in a game against Guinea-Bissau at Durban's Moses Mabhida Stadium.

This wasn't Percy's first game for Bafana Bafana. He had played twice in 2015 during the first round of matches against Angola in the African Cup of Nations but had made very little impact.

Now, at 23 years old, he felt ready. He was in top form, and he felt sure that he could take his goalscoring ability to national level.

Bafana Bafana were being coached by Owen da Gama for the match against Guinea-Bissau. Da Gama let Percy know that he would be on the bench but that he hoped to use him in the second half, depending on how the match unfolded.

'I'm fine with that, Coach,' said Percy. 'I'm

just happy to be part of the national squad. Put me wherever you need me.'

'They told me you'd become a team player, and I'm glad to see that's true,' the coach replied.

On arrival in Durban to meet up with the team, Percy was thrilled to bump into his old teammate Keagan Dolly at the airport. Keagan had recently left Sundowns to play in Europe. Percy had missed having the skilful footballer working alongside him and looked forward to playing with him in the upcoming game.

'Long time no see, Keagan,' he shouted across the busy terminal.

'Too long, Percy. What's happening?' replied Keagan.

On the short journey to the hotel, the two friends discussed what had been happening in each other's lives and what it was like to play in Europe.

Percy loved Durban. Once he'd checked into the hotel, he walked down to the beachfront and soaked up the relaxing vibes, before reporting for training a few hours later.

ROAD TO GLORY

A few hours before the game, when he walked into the changing room and saw the famous gold and yellow outfit hanging in front of his locker, Percy felt a lump in his throat. He was glad to be wearing sunglasses; at least the other players wouldn't notice his emotion.

Getting changed quickly, he thought about how impossible a game with Bafana Bafana had seemed to him a few months ago. His mother liked to say that sometimes dreams come true when you least expect it, and she was right.

As he sang the national anthem from the side of the pitch, he promised himself that if he had a chance to play later, he would make an impact on the game.

The visiting team started well, mounting attack after attack on the Bafana goals, but keeper Itumeleng Khune managed to keep them out. It was a nervous start for Bafana, but the team soon settled.

Thulani Serero collected a long ball through the middle, turned and ran hard at the defence. He was brought down just inside the penalty area and the referee pointed at the penalty spot. Kermit Erasmus, who took the penalty, calmly stroked the ball beyond the goalkeeper's extended fingers to score Bafana's first goal of the match.

Percy sat on the bench for nearly an hour while all the action took place on the field. He was beginning to think his chance wouldn't come, but early in the second half Coach Da Gama turned and signalled to him to get ready. Percy stripped down quickly and took his place on the touchline. The manager called for Erasmus to be replaced and Percy sprinted onto the field to the cheers of the passionate crowd.

No sooner was Percy on the field than a chance presented itself. His team put together a series of beautiful passes, slowly working the ball up the field. Percy spotted a gap and ran for it, and Serero slid the ball into his path. Percy turned and fired low and hard for the corner and watched in amazement as it flew into the back of the net.

GOAL! 2–0 to Bafana Bafana and Percy's

first international goal. What a moment! He ran over to the sideline, lifted his arms in triumph and was swamped by his teammates.

'You did it, Percy! You did it!' shouted Keagan over the roar of the crowd. Percy felt a wave of relief. Any nervousness he'd felt about playing at this level quickly vanished. He was meant to be here.

The newly energised South Africans pressed forward, earning another penalty, which Andile Jali slotted easily into the goals. Guinea-Bissau scored right before the end and the game finished 3–1 to South Africa.

Later that month, Percy found a video clip of his goal on YouTube. He watched it over and over to remind himself that he belonged on the international stage. There would be no stopping him now.

CHAPTER 16

THE GOALS START TO FLOW

Pitso Mosimane had seen Percy's game against Guinea-Bissau for Bafana Bafana and he liked it. He wanted that for Sundowns.

So, Percy began a period of intense training with Coach Mosimane. They watched games together, discussed tactics and spoke on the phone. They spent hours on the training field, working on his speed and decision-making, and developing his killer instinct in front of the goal.

Percy imagined that this was what it was like to have a father. He welcomed the attention and flourished.

The talent-packed team were all working well together, and they liked each other. Sibusiso Vilakazi, Themba Zwane and Khama Billiat felt almost like brothers to Percy. They had played together for so long that they knew what to expect and how to bring out the best in each other.

When the 2017/2018 season kicked off, Mamelodi Sundowns were expected to challenge superstar teams like Orlando Pirates and Kaizer Chiefs for the Premier Soccer League trophy. As runners-up from the previous season, they knew they were good enough to win.

Whenever he had time off, Percy would catch up with Dumisani and Mogau. Dumisani had become an important part of the Royal Eagles FC, while Mogau was playing regularly for Polokwane City. Those face-to-face hours with his siblings were very precious to him. They understood his life and the pressures that he was under.

Off the field, the brothers would do anything for each other. But when they were playing in opposing teams, they were fierce rivals, as they had been since they were children.

Percy couldn't help worrying that he would lose the ability to score goals that he had discovered last season. But the goals kept

THE GOALS START TO FLOW

flowing easily, and the team was looking great.

Percy had grown as a person and as a player. It wasn't all about personal glory any more. He celebrated when a teammate scored, and he felt just as satisfied when he helped set up a goal as when he scored one himself. The result for the team was the important thing.

The whole team played in a tight unit and the strategy was working. After a few games, they had won enough points to be number one in the Champions League table, and game after game they kept up the pressure. By the time the season ended in May 2018, Sundowns had won 18 games, drawn six and lost six, and they were leading by five points. It was an impressive record and the whole club was happy.

Percy had scored 11 goals in the season, which tied with Rodney Ramagalela from Polokwane City and was three more than his teammate Khama Billiat had scored.

'You're becoming a complete striker, Percy,' said Coach Mosimane during training one day. 'Goals from in the box, outside the box, with the head, from open play, set pieces … all of it.'

'Thanks to you, Coach,' said Percy.

Coach Mosimane looked seriously at him. 'You should know that after a season like this, things are probably going to change for you.'

'What do you mean?' asked Percy.

'The international scouts are watching our leagues, Percy. They're looking for bargains. Nobody has contacted me yet, but I want you to be prepared. When that kind of attention comes, it can be overwhelming and it's hard to stay grounded.'

Percy listened to what his coach said, but he didn't really believe it. He was happy at Sundowns. This season had been a good one and the next season would be even better.

CHAPTER 17

TRAGEDY STRIKES

When his phone rang one day, and his brother Dumisani's number showed, Percy expected it to be another happy family call.

'Dumi! How are you, my brother?'

Silence on the line.

'Dumi? Are you there?'

When Dumisani spoke, Percy barely recognised his voice. 'It's Mogau, Percy. Our brother. He's … he's gone.'

Percy didn't understand. How could this be? He had spoken to Mogau only the other day.

Gradually, Dumi explained that their brother had been driving home when he was involved in a car crash that had taken his life.

'Does Mama know?' asked Percy.

'Not yet. I'm going to phone her next.'

'I'll leave now to be with her,' Percy said. He

was devastated. He sat staring into space, hoping and praying to wake up from this nightmare. But it wasn't a dream.

He finally got up and made his way to his car. Nothing made sense. He told no one he was leaving. All he knew was that he had to be there for his mother.

When he arrived at the family home that evening, most of the house was dark. A single light shone in the living room window, but no visitors seemed to be there. Percy was glad about that. He didn't think he could face anyone now. He had to be strong for his mother and for Mogau, even though his heart was breaking.

Percy knocked gently and waited for the door to open. After a few moments, he heard his mother's voice asking who was there.

'It's me, Mama. It's Percy,' he replied.

She opened the door, trying to be brave, but with one look he could tell that she was shattered.

'I got here as soon as I could,' he said and gathered her up in his arms with a big hug. His

TRAGEDY STRIKES

mother said nothing, but just sobbed quietly into Percy's shoulder, and the two of them stood in silence. They had been robbed of a brother and a son, and nothing they could say would change that.

In the following days, the family gathered to share their pain and their memories of Mogau. Everyone remembered him as being one of the friendliest people that they knew. He was always there with a smile and a kind word, no matter whom he was speaking to.

During the funeral the family was comforted by the community's outpouring of love and support. From the outside, it looked like Elizabeth was coping with the situation, but her children could see that she was struggling.

After the funeral, Percy had to go back to Chloorkop to resume training. When he went to his mother's room to say goodbye, her dignified silence had gone, and her face showed anger.

'What is it, Mama? What are you feeling?'

'You know what I blame, Percy? I blame soccer! That stupid game has robbed me of my boy! It has taken all of you away from me and there is nothing I can do about it! Just take, take, take,' she said, bitterly.

Percy felt terrible for his mother. But once she had expressed that emotion, she became calm. She got off her bed, kissed her son goodbye and closed the door to her room. With sadness in his heart, Percy said goodbye to his friends and the rest of his family. He had to go back to his life of football.

CHAPTER 18

THE MIGHTY BARCELONA

On one autumn afternoon in 2018, the whole Sundowns squad gathered in one of the large meeting rooms at the Sundowns offices. There was a buzz in the air. For weeks, they had been told there was something special being discussed, but nobody could guess what it was.

Percy arrived as the club's owner, Patrice Motsepe, was congratulating the players and the coach on the amazing season that they had just experienced. He slid into his seat and hoped that no one had noticed he was late.

'So, let me get to the point. I know you are all holding your breath to hear what we have planned.'

There was a ripple of laughter around the room.

'It's no secret that I think this is the greatest

soccer team in the world,' said Motsepe and everyone cheered.

'And how do we know we are the best?' he asked.

'We beat the best!' shouted someone from the front row.

'That's right. We beat the best. That's why I'm thrilled to tell you that I have invited the world-famous Barcelona Football Club to face the African champions Mamelodi Sundowns Football Club in the Nelson Mandela Centenary Cup at the FNB Stadium.

There was stunned silence for a few moments as everyone digested the news. Barcelona? The actual Barcelona, arguably the best team of all time? Then a cheer started, which got louder and louder.

Percy could hardly believe it, either. Messi, Suárez, Neymar and Dembélé were players that everyone in that room looked up to. What an opportunity to measure himself against the best!

Coach Mosimane told them that Barcelona would fly into Johannesburg on the morning of the match, play at the FNB Stadium in the afternoon and then fly out that evening.

Khama Billiat came over to Percy after the presentation.

'Can you believe it? We're playing Barça … it's going to be insane!'

'Do you think they'll bring their best players, or their second team?' asked Percy.

'Their top guys are coming, man. I heard Coach saying so.'

The next few days passed in a blur. Percy was quite glad that the game had been announced just before it was due to happen. There wasn't long to wait, and no one had time to get too nervous.

In the changing room before the game, Coach Mosimane gave the team a reality check. 'Guys, this is a friendly game and it's only a few days before the World Cup in Russia. Take it easy out there. Enjoy the game. I don't want to see any injuries. You don't want to be known as the player who ruined Messi's World Cup.'

The team laughed but they got the point.

ROAD TO GLORY

The stadium was full, the fans were here to see their idols play and they should not let the game get ugly.

Percy found it hard to believe he wasn't dreaming as he lined up before the match and shook hands with Barcelona captain Andrés Iniesta, legendary forward Lionel Messi and the other world-class players in the team.

When they took to the pitch, Messi stayed on the bench. Percy hoped he would get a chance to play against him later.

Suddenly, the game was on. Sundowns knew they were supposed to treat it like any other game, but it was hard to settle in and they were soon punished. Ousmane Dembélé cut inside in the second minute of the match and delivered an unstoppable shot with his left foot. They realised they had better pull their game together if they didn't want to be humiliated.

Percy was forced to watch most of the opening action, but eventually Sundowns played the ball forward. He found a bit of space and suddenly had the ball at his feet. He ran hard

THE MIGHTY BARCELONA

at the defence and got through, with only the goalkeeper to beat. Percy tried to chip the ball over the keeper, but it didn't work.

He was angry with himself for not doing better and threw himself back into the attack, but Barcelona were solid in defence. When they released Luis Suárez down the line a few minutes later, he calmly slotted the ball into the goals. Barcelona was leading 2–0 after 20 minutes.

The Sundowns fans were worried, but they didn't need to be. For the rest of the first half, the team pushed back strongly, proving that they were good enough to be there and to be taken seriously.

In the seventy-fourth minute of the match, Messi walked onto the pitch, to a huge cheer from the crowd. This is what they wanted to see, and Percy was thrilled to be on the same field as the world's greatest player.

With only a few minutes to go, Sibusiso Vilakazi got one back for Sundowns and the game finished 3–1 to Barcelona. The players were a little disappointed, but there was no shame in losing by two goals to Barcelona. Anyway, it was all about honouring Madiba and delivering a good game for the fans, and that is exactly what they had done.

That game was something that each player would remember and treasure for the rest of his life.

CHAPTER 19

FOOTBALLER OF THE SEASON

When Percy finished the 2017/2018 season as joint top goalscorer in South Africa alongside Rodney Ramagalela, he couldn't have been prouder. He had been named PSL Footballer of the Season and received the Player's Player of the Season award. His team had won the South African Premier League as well as the CAF Champions League trophy. Pitso Mosimane had been named Coach of the Season.

So, although the death of his brother still overshadowed the year and left Percy feeling sad, life had moved on. The next season was the last one on his Sundowns contract and he was expecting it to be even better than the last.

One day his agent, Mmatsatsi Sefalafala, called. 'Are you sitting down, Percy?' she asked.

'Why? What's happened?' said Percy. He

didn't like surprise phone calls after what had happened to Mogau.

'It's good news. Very good. We've received an offer from a Premier League club that would like you to join them next year.'

'Premier League? English Premier League?' Percy repeated, feeling a bit stupid.

'Yes. Brighton & Hove Albion. They finished fifteenth in the league last year.'

'I know Brighton,' said Percy. 'How do they know me?'

'Are you kidding?' replied Mmatsatsi. 'You're a big star. They have talent scouts all over the world and you had an incredible year, so it makes sense.'

'Wow. What's the offer?' asked Percy.

'It's too early to say, but we're looking at about 50 million rand for you to join them.'

Percy felt the blood drain from his face. He thought back to what Coach Mosimane had said to him a few months earlier about preparing himself for the big time. He was pretty sure that he hadn't prepared correctly.

FOOTBALLER OF THE SEASON

'Hello? Percy? Are you there?'

'I'm here, Mmatsatsi. This is a lot to take in. I'll speak to you later.'

Percy felt dizzy. Fifty million rand! That would change not only his life, but his whole family's life, forever. If it happened, it would be the biggest transfer fee to take place in South Africa. A new record.

In the following weeks, Percy received more offers from French, German and Spanish clubs as well, and he grew used to the fact that he would be playing football overseas the next season. He was excited by the challenge and hungry to represent his country in front of the world. There hadn't been a South African in the Premier League for years, and Percy wanted to put that right.

Things were quiet at Sundowns during the off-season. Most of the players trained by themselves to stay in shape before they returned for pre-season training. Percy felt frustrated as, day after day and week after week, he heard no further news about his transfer.

ROAD TO GLORY

Eventually he reached out to his old teammate Keagan, who was now playing for Montpellier in France. Keagan knew exactly what Percy was going through. When he had received his offer to play in Europe, Sundowns had not been keen to release him from his contract, and eventually he'd had to use lawyers.

'You're going to have to fight for this if it's what you want, Percy. They're not going to make it easy,' he warned.

Percy became even more worried a few days later, when he found out that Sundowns had rejected an offer for Khama Billiat to play overseas. Khama was furious and was determined to leave, so a few days later, he went on a free transfer to Kaizer Chiefs.

Percy decided that he was going to have to make it happen. He studied all the clubs that had made offers, and then chose Brighton as the club for him. He told Mmatsatsi Sefalafala, who told the Sundowns managers, and then they waited. But still: nothing.

Percy's frustration grew, and the media were

not helping either. Every day, the newspapers and magazines were full of stories speculating on whether he was leaving or staying with Sundowns and what it all meant. And then, one day, news came that Sundowns was close to signing a Venezuelan striker, José Alí Meza, onto the team for the upcoming season. What did that mean? Was it a sign that they would let Percy go and take on a new striker? He simply didn't know.

Pre-season training was only a few days away and Percy was desperate for some clarity. He knew that Brighton were getting anxious, and he lay awake at night worrying that the offer would be withdrawn. His fitness began to suffer.

On 9 July 2018, the morning that the Sundowns team were supposed to travel to Rustenburg for a training camp, Percy woke up early with a knot in his stomach. He hated all the rumours that were swirling around him, but he had come this far and there was no turning back.

Percy had huge respect for Coach Mosimane,

and he hated to let him down, but he had to think about his future. He wrote out a message on his phone, then deleted it, then tried another one, then deleted it … over and over until he thought it was right. Finally, he found a respectful, but firm, way of saying that he was not available for the training camp. It was one of the hardest things he had ever had to do, but he needed to show that he was serious. He waited for hours for a reply from the coach, but it never came.

Sundowns were flying to Togo to kick off their CAF Champions League games on 17 July. Percy knew that he needed to have an answer by then.

CHAPTER 20

A NEW DAWN

Percy spotted his agent in a corner at the back of the restaurant when he arrived for the meeting. Mmatsatsi Sefalafala stood up and they fist-bumped as he approached.

'So?' Percy asked, sitting down.

'Good news.'

'Oh! Thank goodness.' Percy was relieved. There could only be one piece of good news. The deal was going through.

'But there's a catch. She looked at him sternly. 'The club would like an apology first. From you.'

'An apology? For what?'

'For leaking the transfer news to the media, and thereby creating a media frenzy,' his agent answered. 'And for skipping the training camp.'

'I didn't leak the news. People talk. That's not my fault!'

'That's not important, Percy. We need to move past all of this.'

Just then the waitress arrived to take their order. Percy was silent, looking out the window onto the suburban parking lot, where he'd parked his beautiful car with his name on it, donated by his sponsors. He sighed heavily.

His first instinct was to fight back and to proclaim his innocence. But was an apology so bad? After all, he had missed the training camp. He hadn't 'leaked' the story, he had just answered a question when a reporter had asked, but still … what did it matter? If the club wanted him to say sorry, he could do it.

'Sure, no problem. Set it up and I'll be there.'

'Really?' asked Mmatsatsi. 'I was expecting you to be outraged.'

'It's fine. I want to move on with my life. And I'm sure they do, too.'

His agent was pleased. 'Great, Percy, great! The signing will be quick and easy and then the sky's the limit.'

Later that day, Percy got a message to come

to the Sundowns offices to meet with the management team. He dressed in a suit, called an Uber from home, and made the familiar journey back to the club.

Arriving there a few minutes early, a flood of emotion surprised Percy as he walked into the lobby. For years, Sundowns had been his home, his inspiration and the place that had changed his life. He knew how much he owed to everyone in this building, and he was sorry that things had turned a little sour in the past weeks.

But Percy was also aware that he had contributed to Sundowns' success. He walked over to the secretary's desk, feeling that he could stand tall.

He was immediately shown into the boardroom, where Coach Mosimane and Patrice Motsepe were waiting. They offered Percy coffee and sat down to chat.

Percy had known these men since he was a teenager. Looking into their faces, he was reminded of how much they had believed and invested in him and nurtured his career.

'I'm sorry for how this has gone over the last few weeks,' Percy broke the silence. 'It wasn't my intention at all, and I hope you know that.'

'Thank you for saying that,' said Coach Mosimane. 'I believe you.'

Percy explained to them what had been going on from his side, and the two older men also explained the different things they had been juggling and decisions they'd had to make. Percy realised how complicated running a football club can be.

After a few minutes, the tension in the room evaporated and at the end of the discussion, the coach thanked Percy for his service to Mamelodi Sundowns.

On the way home, Percy heard a report on the radio saying that they had reached an agreement and that Percy Tau was leaving Mamelodi Sundowns.

CHAPTER 21

OVERSEAS

Flying business class was something Percy could get used to. The flight from Johannesburg to London passed by so quickly that he didn't even get a chance to enjoy everything. He hoped to be able to do it again soon.

A driver was waiting to pick him up from Heathrow Airport, and Percy settled in for the drive down to the city of Brighton, on the south coast of England.

He chatted to the driver for part of the way, but he must have dozed off because the next thing he knew, the driver had stopped the car and opened his door.

'Welcome to the Training Centre of Brighton & Hove Albion, Mr Tau,' the man said with pride in his voice. He picked up Percy's bags and showed him into the reception area.

ROAD TO GLORY

Percy looked around in awe. For the first time, he realised what a different world he was entering.

'Percy! Is that you? Welcome to the club!' shouted a voice from across the room. Percy turned to see the owner of the club, Tony Bloom, walking towards him with his hand thrust out. Percy shook it and relaxed briefly. He felt he was in the right place.

Bloom walked Percy around the facility and explained what and where everything was. It felt like a different universe. There were 11 full- and half-sized pitches, an indoor pitch, accommodation for the first team and the youth squads, a medical room, a gymnasium and state-of-the-art media facilities. It was all very impressive.

As they walked around, Bloom introduced Percy to various people and laid out his plans for the club. Recently Bloom had purchased a second club in Belgium called Union Saint-Gilloise. Percy had never heard of them before, but Bloom explained that USG had once been

'Welcome to the Training Centre of Brighton & Hove Albion!'

powerful before falling on hard times and dropping into the Belgian Second Division. Bloom was investing heavily in their staff, players and facilities in a bid to make them one of the greats again.

'With your help, Percy, USG will be promoted back into the First Division at the end of the season.'

Percy was confused. 'You're transferring me already?'

Bloom laughed. 'Nothing could be further from the truth. We're loaning you to the club on a mission to get them promoted. It'll be good for your transition into European football. It'll guarantee you game time while we sort out your English work permit and, speaking personally, I need you there.'

Percy struggled to hide his disappointment. He knew that he still did not have the correct papers to play in England, but he had expected to be training with Brighton while he waited. This was not part of his plan. But he was a professional, so he nodded.

OVERSEAS

'Whatever you need, boss.'

Over the next few days, Percy began to see the logic in Tony Bloom's thinking. The chairman was building a major football franchise and he wanted his players to do the work that was needed. He assured Percy that he would be playing in the English Premier League before long.

So, Percy set off on the next leg of his journey to Brussels, the capital city of Belgium. As he drove through the beautiful streets, a feeling of calm settled over him. He could get used to this. And when he arrived at the club to see that his team were dressed in yellow and blue, just like his beloved Sundowns, it felt like home.

Percy had realised that he enjoyed studying and that football wasn't going to last forever, so he had decided to enrol to do a BCom degree through the University of South Africa while he was in Brussels. It kept him busy when he wasn't training; and, of course, his mother was delighted when she heard the news.

After a few weeks of training, Percy played

his first game for his new club in the Croky Cup, against a team called City Pirates. Percy didn't know much about the opposition, but the level of talent and commitment in his team had convinced him that this was the right place to be.

Out on the pitch, he prowled the penalty area, waiting for a chance to show what he could do. USG played well and scored first, then added a second goal to end the first half 2–0. Percy was pleased, but he wanted to leave a mark. He needed to be patient.

With only a few moments left in the second half of the game, his team gathered the ball deep in their ranks and pressed forward. Then a quick one-two between the midfield players saw the ball squeeze past the defence and towards the edge of the penalty area. Percy turned and darted towards it, looking up to see the goalkeeper also rushing towards the ball.

Percy got there first and, without even thinking about it, controlled the ball on his left foot, and stabbed it forward, chipping it high

OVERSEAS

into the air, above the goalkeeper's outstretched hands. It arced upwards, landed, bounced once and rolled into the back of the net.

GOAL!

His teammates rushed towards him as the goalkeeper picked himself up and walked slowly towards the net.

'Mate, that was one of the best goals I've ever seen,' said the midfielder Marcel Mehlem.

'How did you do that, Percy? Unbelievable!' another USG player exclaimed, just before Percy was smothered in hugs.

Standing on a field in Belgium, thousands of kilometres from where he had grown up, Percy suddenly realised that no matter where he was, his team was his family and the soccer pitch was his home. This Second Division game in Belgium was part of a bigger journey that he was on.

Percy's goal was to keep representing his country on the international stage. As long as he had a ball at his feet and teammates around him, he knew he was going in the right direction.

SOURCES

https://citizen.co.za/phakaaathi/south-africa-soccer-phakaaathi-phakaaathi/984965/984965/

https://en.wikipedia.org/wiki/2017%E2%80%9318_South_African_Premier_Division

https://www.businesslive.co.za/bd/sport/soccer/2018-07-05-brighton-offer-record-amount-for-percy-tau/

https://www.iol.co.za/pretoria-news/news/pitsos-grand-plan-for-percy-12804762

https://www.iol.co.za/pretoria-news/the-life-and-resurrection-of-percy-tau-14779818

https://www.iol.co.za/sport/soccer/psl/how-percy-tau-went-from-slacker-to-superstar-at-mamelodi-sundowns-14785377

https://www.politicalanalysis.co.za/english-club-brighton-albion-announce-percy-taus-belgian-loan-move/

https://www.soccerladuma.co.za/news/articles/categories/south-africa/from-sundowns-academy-to-caf-cl-winners-1/239300?page=1

SOURCES

https://www.theargus.co.uk/sport/16171372.Albion_owner_Tony_Bloom_on_brink_of_buying_Belgian_club_but_with_no_links_to_Seagulls/?ref=mac

https://www.thesouthafrican.com/mogau-tsehla-polokwane-city-defender-dies-in-a-car-accident/

https://www.thesouthafrican.com/percy-tau-five-quick-fast-about-the-sundowns-superstar/

https://www.timeslive.co.za/sport/soccer/2018-05-31-how-percy-tau-changed-his-mothers-life/

CLASSROOM ACTIVITIES
ORAL ACTIVITIES

1. Role play a conversation between Percy and his mother about choosing soccer as a career. In your conversation, show the differences and similarities between their ideas and opinions. What do they agree and disagree about?

2. From reading the book and your own knowledge of soccer, present a short speech on what Percy Tau's strengths and weaknesses are as a soccer player. You may wish to do some additional research on the internet.

3. Imagine you are Percy and you are talking to a good friend.
   - Describe a typical day in your life.
   - Tell your friend which achievements you

ORAL ACTIVITIES

are most proud of, and why.
- Tell your friend what you have found most difficult in your life, and why.

4. Write a short speech for Percy to give at the 2018 PSL Awards ceremony. In the speech, include some highlights of his career. Remember to thank the key people in his life for what they have done to help him succeed. Present the speech as if you were Percy.

5. Do some research on Mogau Tshehla. Use information from this book and from your research and write an obituary for him. Present the obituary to the class.

WRITTEN ACTIVITIES

In the activities below, remember to follow the writing process:
- Brainstorm your ideas.
- Organise them into paragraphs.
- Write a first draft.
- Revise and edit your draft, correcting grammar and spelling mistakes.
- Write a neat final draft.

1. From the information in the story, create a timeline of Percy Tau's career. Make a poster of the timeline and decorate it with pictures of some of the highlights.

2. Imagine you are Percy at the time of his brother Mogau's death. Write a poem to express how you feel.

3. Which soccer game in the story did you find

WRITTEN ACTIVITIES

most exciting? Write an email or a letter to a relative or friend, describing the game as if you were there. Explain why you enjoyed it.

4. Read the last half of Chapter 19 again. Write the message that Percy wrote to Coach Mosimane explaining why he was not available for the training camp. Make sure that you get the tone of the message right.

5. Various people supported Percy as he built his career. Each person played a different role in helping him develop his skills as a player or develop himself as a person.
   - Write a list of the people who were important in Percy's development.
   - Next to each name describe what that person did to help him.
   - Compare your list with a friend's.

AUTHOR'S NOTE

The events in this book about Percy Tau are based on fact. However, I have taken creative licence in certain scenes with dialogue and some detail, in the interests of creating a story that is entertaining and fun for young readers. A few of the minor characters are fictional. I have tried to stay true to the character and life story of my subject, based on the known facts.

ALSO AVAILABLE IN THE
ROAD TO GLORY
SERIES